3\3\15

SCIENCE EXPLORER

JUNIOR

JUNIOR SCIENTISTS

Experiment with Magnets

by Christine Taylor-Butler

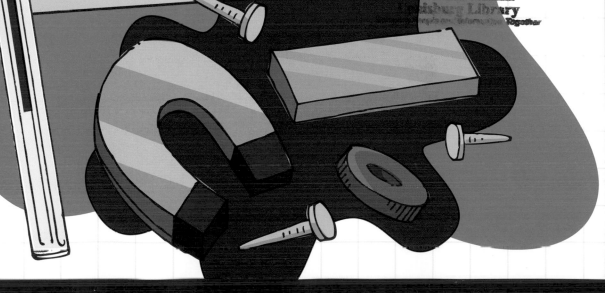

CHERRY LAKE PUBLISHING · ANN ARBOR, MICHIGAN

NOTE TO PARENTS AND TEACHERS: Please review the instructions for these experiments before your children do them. Be sure to help them with any experiments you do not think they can safely conduct on their own.

NOTE TO KIDS: Be sure to ask an adult for help with these experiments. Always put your safety first!

CHERRY LAKE Publishing

Published in the United States of America by Cherry Lake Publishing
Ann Arbor, Michigan
www.cherrylakepublishing.com

Content Editor: Robert Wolffe, EdD, Professor of Teacher Education, Bradley University, Peoria, Illinois
Reading Adviser: Cecilia Minden-Cupp, PhD, Literacy Consultant

Design and Illustration: The Design Lab

Photo Credits: Page 11, ©iStockphoto.com/LifeJourneys; page 15, ©PhotosToGo.com; page 21, ©Moth/Dreamstime.com; page 22, ©Phil Degginger/Alamy; page 23, ©iStockphoto.com/Beisea; page 27, ©iStockphoto.com/Tommounsey; page 29, ©iStockphoto.com/jarenwicklund

Library of Congress Cataloging-in-Publication Data
Taylor-Butler, Christine.
  Junior scientists. Experiment with magnets / by Christine Taylor-Butler.
     p. cm.–(Science explorer junior)
  Includes bibliographical references and index.
  ISBN-13: 978-1-60279-844-1 (lib. bdg.)
  ISBN-10: 1-60279-844-3 (lib. bdg.)
  1. Magnetism—Experiments—Juvenile literature. 2. Science projects—Juvenile literature. I. Title. II. Title: Experiment with magnets. III. Series.
  QC753.7.T39 2010
  538.078–dc22   2009048833

Portions of the text have previously appeared in *Super Cool Science Experiments: Magnets* published by Cherry Lake Publishing.

Cherry Lake Publishing would like to acknowledge the work of The Partnership for 21st Century Skills. Please visit *www.21stcenturyskills.org* for more information.

Printed in the United States of America
Corporate Graphics Inc.
July 2010
CLFA07

TABLE OF CONTENTS

Let's Experiment!

Experiments
are fun!

Have you ever done a science **experiment**? They
can be lots of fun! You can use experiments to
learn about almost anything.

Good scientists observe the world around them.

This book will help you learn how to think like a scientist. Scientists have a special way of learning new things. Some people call it the Scientific Method. This is how it often works:

• Scientists notice things. They **observe** the world around them. They ask questions about things they see, hear, taste, touch, or smell. They come up with problems they would like to solve.

A scientist guesses what the answer to her question is.

- They gather information. They use what they already know to guess the answers to their questions. This kind of guess is called a **hypothesis**.

• Then they test their ideas. They perform experiments or build models. They watch and write down what happens. They learn from each new test.

- They think about what they learned and reach a **conclusion**. This means they come up with an answer to their question. Sometimes they **conclude** that they need to do more experiments!

When a scientist figures out the answer to her question, she has reached a conclusion.

Conclusion

You will need both horseshoe and bar magnets for the experiments in this book.

We will use the scientific method to learn more about magnets. Each experiment will teach us something new. Are you ready to be a scientist?

Let the Force Be with You!

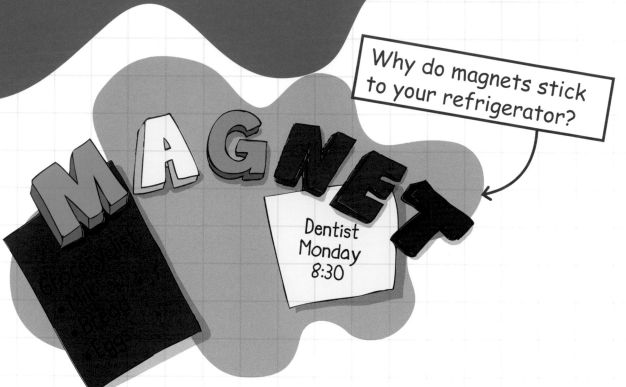

Why do magnets stick to your refrigerator?

First, we need to gather information. What do you know about magnets? You may know that magnets stick to things. Are there magnets stuck on your refrigerator? This is because the door is made of metal. Magnets are **attracted** to some kinds of metal.

Do you think magnets are attracted to other things? Let's do an experiment to find out. Choose a hypothesis:

1. Magnets are only attracted to some metals.
2. Magnets are also attracted to other things.

Let's get started!

Magnets can be very useful!

Here's what you'll need:

- Paper and a pencil to write down what you see
- A magnet
- A paperclip
- A stamp
- A rubber band
- A small rock
- A piece of paper
- An eraser

Collect your supplies.

Does Attract	Does Not Attract

Does the magnet attract the paperclip?

Instructions:

1. Draw a line down the middle of your paper. There should now be two parts. Write "Does Attract" at the top of the left section. Write "Does Not Attract" at the top of the right section.

2. Place the magnet on top of the paperclip and lift up. Does the paperclip stick to the magnet? If so, write "paperclip" in the left section. If not, write it in the right section.

3. Repeat these steps with the stamp, rubber band, paper, and rock.

Does the magnet attract the stamp or rock?

Conclusion:

Look at the two parts in your notebook. Which objects were attracted to the magnet? Which ones were not? Did you find that the magnet would only attract the paperclip? What does that tell you about magnets? Magnets can only attract items that are made of metal.

Magnets attract all kinds of things made of metal.

Do Opposites Really Attract?

A bar magnet is marked with an "N" and an "S."

Take a close look at a bar magnet. One end is marked with an "N." The other end is marked with an "S." These letters mark the north and south poles of the magnet. Every magnet has two poles. Each pole acts in a different way.

We know that magnets are attracted to metals. We also know that magnets are made of metal. What do you think happens when you put two magnets next to each other? Do you think it matters if the N and S are touching? Does it matter if they are not touching? An experiment can help answer these questions. Choose a hypothesis:

1. Magnets attract each other.
2. Magnets do not attract each other.

Let's get started!

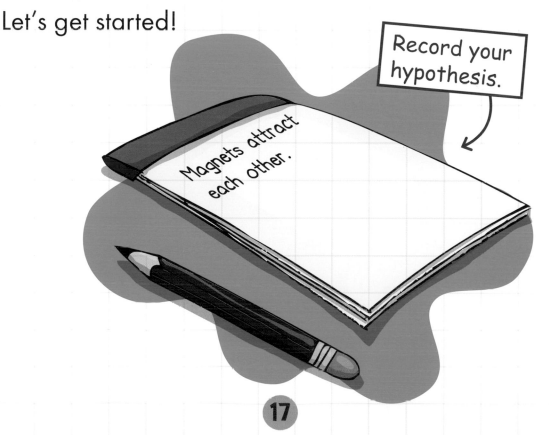

Record your hypothesis.

Magnets attract each other.

Here's what you'll need:

- 2 bar magnets with ends marked "S" and "N"
- Paper and a pencil to write down what you see

Instructions:

1. Put the bar magnets on the table in front of you. Place the "S" end of the first magnet next to the "N" end of the second magnet. What happens? Write it down.

What happens when you place the "S" and the N" next to each other?

2. Slowly move the two "N" ends toward each other. Now what happens? Try pushing them together. Can you do it?

3. Try to put the two ends marked "S" together. Do you get the same results? What do you think this means?

Conclusion:

Sometimes an experiment does not give us a simple yes or no. Magnets repel each other when you try to put two poles of the same kind together. Opposite poles attract each other. That means both of our possible hypotheses were correct!

Magnets are used to hook these toy train cars together.

Share the Power

Some small magnets can lift big things!

We have already seen that magnets can stick to objects when they touch. Magnets can be very powerful, though. Do you think it is possible for magnets to attract things without touching them?

Let's find out. Choose a hypothesis:

1. Magnets can only attract items by touching them.
2. Magnets can attract items without touching them.

Let's get started!

Magnets come in many shapes and sizes.

Here's what you'll need:

- A magnet
- Several paperclips
- A pencil and paper to write down what you see

Collect your supplies.

Instructions:

1. Set a paperclip down on a table.

2. Slowly lower your magnet toward the paperclip. What happens as the magnet gets closer to the paperclip?

3. Take a paperclip and stick it to the magnet.
4. Now take another paperclip and touch it to the one on the magnet. What happens? What happens when you add a third paperclip? How many paperclips can you link together?

How many paperclips can you link together?

Conclusion:

Did you prove your hypothesis? Did you find that your magnet attracted the paperclip? Did you also find that a paperclip touching a magnet can attract other paperclips? This happens because a magnet can transfer its force through pieces of metal. Stronger magnets can transfer magnetic force through more things and bigger things!

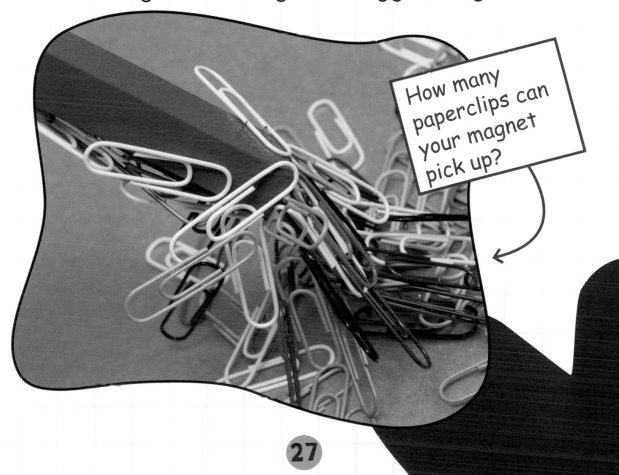

How many paperclips can your magnet pick up?

Do It Yourself!

What other questions do you have about magnets?

Okay, scientists! You learned that magnets are only attracted to metal. You also learned that opposite poles of magnets attract each other. Finally, you learned that magnets can attract objects without touching them. You learned by thinking like a scientist.

Maybe now you are wondering if magnets attract all kinds of metal. You might wonder if you can make your own magnets. What are you waiting for? Use your science skills to find the answers to your questions!

Write down your ideas for more experiments with magnets.

attracted (uh-TRAK-ted) drawn toward

conclude (kuhn-KLOOD) to make a final decision based on what you know

conclusion (kuhn-KLOO-zhuhn) a final decision, thought, or opinion

experiment (ecks-PARE-uh-ment) a scientific way to test a guess about something

hypothesis (hy-POTH-uh-sihss) using what you know to make a guess about what will happen in an experiment

observe (ob-ZURV) to see something or notice things by using the other senses

repel (ruh-PELL) push away

FOR MORE INFORMATION

BOOKS

Jeffers, Fred. Mondo *Magnets: 40 Attractive (and Repulsive) Devices & Demonstrations*. Chicago: Chicago Review Press, 2007.

Royston, Angela. *Magnetic and Nonmagnetic*. Chicago: Heinemann Library, 2009.

WEB SITES

Magnet Lab: Try This at Home
www.magnet.fsu.edu/education/students/activities/ trythisathome.html
Try these fun experiments with magnets.

Magnet Man: Cool Experiments with Magnets
www.coolmagnetman.com/magindex.htm
Learn more about magnets and magnet safety.

INDEX

ABOUT THE AUTHOR

Christine Taylor-Butler is a freelance author with degrees in both civil engineering and art and design from the Massachusetts Institute of Technology (MIT). When she is not writing, she is reading, drawing, or looking for unusual new science ideas to write about. She is the author of more than 40 fiction and nonfiction books for children.